MANHATTAN MELODY

MANHATTAN MELODY

Patricia Faith Polak

Copyright © 2017 Patricia Faith Polak.

All rights reserved. No part of this book may be used or reproduced by any means, graphic, electronic, or mechanical, including photocopying, recording, taping or by any information storage retrieval system without the written permission of the author except in the case of brief quotations embodied in critical articles and reviews.

Archway Publishing books may be ordered through booksellers or by contacting:

Archway Publishing
1663 Liberty Drive
Bloomington, IN 47403
www.archwaypublishing.com
1 (888) 242-5904

Because of the dynamic nature of the Internet, any web addresses or links contained in this book may have changed since publication and may no longer be valid. The views expressed in this work are solely those of the author and do not necessarily reflect the views of the publisher, and the publisher hereby disclaims any responsibility for them.

Any people depicted in stock imagery provided by Thinkstock are models, and such images are being used for illustrative purposes only. Certain stock imagery © Thinkstock.

ISBN: 978-1-4808-5386-7 (sc)
ISBN: 978-1-4808-5387-4 (hc)
ISBN: 978-1-4808-5388-1 (e)

Library of Congress Control Number: 2017916667

Print information available on the last page.

Archway Publishing rev. date: 11/14/2017

DEDICATION

To: Emil J.
Always Believer

Cliffie
brother taken by leukemia
Inspiring Angel

Donald
once physics major
Haunting brotherly part of me

ACKNOWLEDGMENTS

For my parents: Ruth Barbara and Joseph Patrick Leuzzi
You gave a legacy of words, and
fashioned me a debutante

Ever gratitude for the refined intellect of Sister Dorothy Mercedes of the Sisters of St. Joseph, debating coach at The Mary Louis Academy. Kudos to those dauntless ones, ever tried to teach me to sit a saddle. Exuberant riding in the Moscow Hippodrome, and being part of a Polish wedding on horseback. (Jumping Captain Protein!) A modicum of political science in the classroom at Trinity College, Washington, DC, and on Capitol Hill. Worked in the world of finance. If no fulsome pension from the years with Brahmin John Train, inculcated to write a lyric with "strong muscular verbs." Enormous indebtedness for the academic welcome given at SUNY Empire, and the many kindnesses shown by alumni administrator, Toby Tobrocke—veritably life changing. From Manhattanville's Master's program, an experience in erudition and elegance, Suzannah Lessard; and tragically passed too soon, the exceptional mind of John Herman.

Thanks to friends extraordinary in their own rights—Mimi Leahey and her highly talented spouse Scott Nangle, Portia Redfield, Linda Sullivan; and cousins Therese Southworth, Carolyn Rose Vadala, and wishing the distance nearer, Paula and Susan Sonnichsen. Heartfelt credit to a brilliant doctor, Daniel Goodman, MD. Truly missed the late Elizabeth 'Libby' Bass and Lucia Capodilupo, PhD. For generosity enabling us to expatriate to Sayville, Long Island, and living space (to work on the novel!), Bill Venegas. Finally, paws, from a Bowser Great Beyond, Ginger and Cupid; and now the rescue felines—Flash and Foxy—think iambs are catnip.

CONTENTS

Practicing One's Craft 1
Zum Zum 3
The Classical Age 5
Write as Rain 7
Tempo of the City 9
Mornings at Seven 11
Nocturne 13
The Bronze 15
Vignettes 17
Allies Day: Childe Hassam 19
Heavy Metal 21
The Boulevardier's Dawn / Cocktail Hour 23
Pictures at an Exhibition: New York City 25
Some Irreparable Loss 27
The Gothamburg Bible 29
Can You Hear Me, Watson? 33
The Gypsy Teakettle 35
Urban Landscape: The Metropolitan Museum 37
Photomontage: Bleecker Street 39
Elegy in a City Boneyard 41
Vincero 43
The World's Oldest Writing in the Trade Tower Holocaust ... 45
The Aberrant Storm 47
Carousel in Winter 49
Toni 51
Buskers 53
Bubble, Bubble 55
The Figure 5 in Gold 57
To Jumble 59

If, by Chance 61
Dolce Far Niente 63
The Saint's Day Party 65
Eight O'Clock 67
The Grasshopper 69
Art Is Not a Brassiere 71
Ne Plus Ultra 73
Reverie 75
Barcarole 77
Urban Homesteading 79
Blizzard Day: New York 81
The Big Bang 83
Our Town 85
The *Brandenburg Concertos:* Snowy Manhattan 87
Twenty-Four-Dollar Real Estate 89
The City Karooms across My Bedroom Wall 91
Portrait 93
Vantage 95
Nighthawks (1942) 97
Ferries 99
Rain Tattoo 101

MANHATTAN MELODY

Of the book's fifty poems, eighteen have been previously published in the following journals.

Art Is Not a Brassiere	*Caveat Lector*
Dolce Far Niente	*Word(s) 77*
The Saint's Day Party	*Forge*
Eight O'Clock	*Inkwell*
Heavy Metal	*Big Scream*
Mornings At Seven	*Land of Compassion* (online)
Nighthawks (1942)	*2 Bridges Review*
Nocturne	*Big Scream*
Portrait	*Land of Compassion* (online)
Some Irreparable Loss	*Big Scream*
The Big Bang	*Word(s) 77*
The Boulevardier's Dawn / Cocktail Hour	*Home Planet News Online*
To Jumble	*2 Bridges Review*
Urban Homesteading	*Great American Poetry Show*
Vantage	*Home Planet News Online*
Vignettes	*Land of Compassion* (online)
Zum Zum	*Wild Violet* (online)
Twenty-Four-Dollar Real Estate	*Land of Compassion* (online)
Ferries	*Collection of the Ellis Island Museum*

INTRODUCTION

With my husband of forty-eight years, it's been a magic carpet ride.

This book includes poems about New York by a native New Yorker. There have been Walt Whitman, Richard Wilbur, Djuna Barnes, Allen Ginsberg, Hettie Jones, and Marie Howe. But this New Yorker has played roulette in Saddam Hussein's Baghdad. *Manhattan looked more sublime, more diverse.* Another time, I quick-talked my husband out of jail by the Black Sea coast, where the Roman poet Ovid was exiled. *New York appeared more myriad in its wonders, contradictions.* And we smuggled a pony-sized bottle of Chartreuse into Muammar Gaddafi's dusty, dry Benghazi, Libya, to celebrate a wedding anniversary. *Returning, New York City was replete with originalities, distinctions.*

While not all my travel has been to obscure and dangerous spots around the globe, this eventful life has given me such appreciation of New York.

To follow, my lyrics on my city.

PRACTICING ONE'S CRAFT

Ocean liners and ferries, fire tugs and yachts—
    axiomatic: this town's an island,
ensconced on Sutton Place, watching
    a barge broach the East River,
a denizen of Riverside Drive voyeuring
    a ketch upon the Hudson,
a dweller in Battery Park City battening on
    a coast guard cutter patrolling
        New York Harbor.

Sculls dip under the Fifty-Ninth Street Bridge with
    a stroke of luck.
Oysters again bed down in the reclaimed
    Hudson River.

Water taxis, day liners, sightseeing boats,
    and sails commingle.
Tankers ply the estuary with sloops
    and flippant Chris-Craft.

Prolific progeny of Henry Hudson's
    Half Moon and Giovanni da Verrazzano's
    La Dauphine,
or, as the RMS *Queen Mary 2*, when you've
    debuted in New York, you're launched.

Sardined on the subway, the city is
    a petrological,
intimate isle, as if 1.6 million castaways
weigh anchor, straphanger; Manhattan's
    pond is not for small fry.

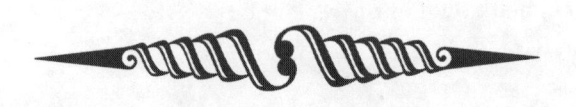

ZUM ZUM

The hot chocolate sipped at Schrafft's,
the nickel's worth of mac and cheese
    at the Automat—
the bygone watering holes that only linger
    in the adipose tissue.
My working life coincided with the launch
    of a wurst purveyor with kraut or not
    and mustards, birch beer, and
    upon tap, *hiel und dunkle.*
Found about Manhattan, one Zum Zum was
    niched in the concourse of the then
    Pan Am Building.
A steady traffic of business types came
    to be served by dirndl-clad waitresses
    in the blond-wood setting on the
    appealing pewter plates and heavy
    glass mugs.
Partake of the pungent crisp of the grilled wurst
    skins, the vinegar of the accompanying
    potato salad.
Before the cell phone and the text message,
    patrons were seen doing the *Times*
    crossword puzzle while munching a
    baurenwurst or chatting a server while
    nibbling a brat.
Zum Zum's stacked decorative tuns of beer—
    this wasn't a martini drinker's hidey-hole—
    Gretchen or Liesl pulled a foamy, and it
    washed down the meal.
Somehow, the *freundlich* was replaced by
    the power lunch or, at the opposite extreme,
    fast food.
We saw the wurst, and it's gotten worst.

THE CLASSICAL AGE

Almost slag, the sooty February remnants of city snow,
anthracite mountain of the building's compacted, bagged
    garbage.
The upscale scavenger of our midden.
Her belted trench coat, slouch-brim hat, aviator wrap
    sunglasses ... only
the accessorizing wheely grocery cart, clown smear of
    red lipstick,
wristlet-length gloves on, she mines the pile for
    aluminum cans,
anemic sunlight as the cart layers the varicolored logos
    of competing soft drinks.
Dribbled embarrassment of detritus into the slush:
    apartment 7K's ripped junk mail, somebody's emptied
    fifth of Absolut, pizza crust with toothy dentation.
And then a glimpse into the woman's head beneath the
    slouch-brim; the filling cart elicits a rictus of
    painted smile
In ancient Athens, the vote to expel from the city by
    casting bits of broken pottery, the *ostraka*, and
    hence our "ostracize."
Here, the supermarket calculates refundable nickels.

WRITE AS RAIN

The tropical steaminess of a late summer's
   cloudburst,
      Manhattan as sauna,
         asphalt bubbly,
            humid, wilting ...
               plonk;
                   city street as caldera ...
                plonk, *plink*.
Tar pit of the construct mammoth.

Sweltering,
   vaporous,
      the rubbery smack of tire track ...
         splash, backsplash,
            slurred traction,
               aquaplane,
                  skidsy.
Step, *splosh*.

TEMPO OF THE CITY

> *A near horizon whose sharp jags*
> *Cut brutally into a sky*
> *Of leaden heaviness, and crags*
> —Amy Lowell, "New York at Night"

A Manhattan moonrise hangs above
    the skyscrapered city
like a snowball tossed by a perturbed Rip Van Winkle.
Flakes stir and fall in the canyons of Wall Street,
    tickertape confetti—crystals as ephemeral as a stock tip.
The storm-covered equestrian statue of the first president
    in Union Square is a horsey snowman.
Pedestrians hunker down behind ski masks and cautiously
    navigate slick sidewalks.
A traffic jam at a slush-soupy corner, and from a car's window
    is heard the radio with the Village People's "YMCA";
most passersby respond to the lyric's up beat and are energized,
some even smiling as they jump the corner's icy pool:
    "Y-M-C-A."
Rhythmic weatherproofing.

MORNINGS AT SEVEN

City blocks with donuteries, druggeries, and dry cleaners;
   air temperate, as if March had rinsed it,
      pounded it against the travertine on skyscrapers
         until it was like a favored pair of jeans.

Urbanites unbundling, turtling out
   from wools and downs,
      the mind itself shedding torpor,
         senses keening, synapses firing.

In the indestructible gingkoes along the avenue
   adjacent to the thrum of traffic,
      a plaint of sparrows, managing in this metropolis,
         the mate and nest mandate.

Talismanic spring light, like Eurydice
   emerging from the underworld—

in front of a florist,
   impervious to the capriciousness
      of the city's seasons,
         flowering quince in a galvanized pail,
            all gossamer orange-pink and cinquefoil petals

tempting a splurge,
   so for a fragile day an indoor garden,
      an unalloyed delight,
         amid the Barnes chairs, dhurries, and Dali lithographs.

NOCTURNE

When the sunset has squandered itself and
    the city's sky deepens to what lyricists call
        indigo,
car lights flash on, weaving ribbon candy:
    headlamps peppermint,
        taillights disappearing cinnamon,
            homebound pedestrians footslogging.

Neon's luciferous
    crazy quilt of signage, billboards
        is intensified by gridlock;
            police/fire/ambulance, frenzied sound and light,
                taxis blinker on- and off-duty,
                    vans spray-painted DayGlo.
Passing buses filling lanes,
    commuters' glazed stares at
        a window dresser's fantasies.
Intersections jammed, horns discord:
    flourishes of automotive
        cornets, flugelhorns, euphonium.
The rampage exhausts eventually.
    Anticipate the moonrise,
        a flimsy disk (dish-faced moon) vying with the
            illuminated metropolitan night.

THE BRONZE

In the sunlight-flooded park where the nannies go,
which overlooks a gentle bend of the East River,

there is a sculpture of a monumental wild boar;
upon his bronze haunch, and mild-miened,

he oversees the prams and strollers,
toddlers, and sturdy-gaited children

out for the air and doing their first socializing,
while the minders observe upon park benches

the eddying river wide across to Queens,
this enclave where ivied bricks screen the luxury high-risers.

Then a boy of about four, with tousled blond hair,
rushes to show his nanny something.

It's possible to make out their conversation is in Creole,
which, coming from the boy, startles and delights.

A nanny's life ... from Haiti, devoted and maternal, now
upon an hourly wage for an urbanite working couple.

But what premium has the child's language skill,
and to what adult adventures may Creole lead him?

Even this moment, the head of tight black curls
bends to the child's flaxen, their obvious bond.

As they speak privately in lilted island French patois,
the big sculptural boar seems to take it all in.

Many small hands have burnished the bronze,
happy to share this plein air scene with the tête-à-tête.

Wild boar sculpture by Pietro Tacca, 1970.

VIGNETTES

Luminescent-green leer
   of blinking
      ordinals,
the casket of a table clock
   spews
      its hornet drone.
Dream fragment
   a vivid instant before
      quicksilvering,
fluttery eyed
   in the warm Abraham's bosom
      of down pillow.

With a flick,
   phosphor of the kitchen fixture
      filaments.
Pad barefoot, quick
   across the slick
      faux marble linoleum.
Pumper thump
   as the faucet streams
      a tepid flow.
Aromatic hubble-bubble
   of the Braun
      elixiring
         morning's coffee.

Kinographic monochrome,
   the slab high-risers,
      unshuttering stores,
acrid twitch
   of fresh newsprint
      in twine-bundled stacks.
Young Yemini
   adroitly penknifes
      and proffers a *Times*,
         one-handed
for the money transaction,
   a felicitation
      at daybreak,
         Shukran.[**]

[**] Arabic for "Thank you."

ALLIES DAY: CHILDE HASSAM

All a poet can do today is warn.
—Wilfred Owen

Painter of flags, intoxicated by them.
Impressionist master of the martial display,
outstanding among the Flag Series, this exultation.
After America's entry into the Great War on April 6,
    the stars and stripes displayed in New York
    alongside the French tricolor
    and the Union Jack,
Hassam adding the Canadian Red Ensign
    to the sun-struck brilliance
at the northeast corner of Fifty-Second Street,
    looking north along Fifth Avenue,
    there by Saint Thomas Church, the University Club,
    the Gotham Hotel, and the Fifth Avenue Presbyterian Church.
Quintessential cityscape, New York City of the noblesse oblige.
Expanse of aqua sky, pedestrian parade below.
Focal point: American flag against the shimmering blue sky
    and the gleam upon the ecclesiastical buildings—
    divine approval for the United States having entered
    the Alliance.
Dazzled, giddy, passionate upon banners,
    variations on red, white, and blue, and this symbolizing
    the unity of the Allies.
The closely applied brushstrokes and Hassam's white impasto
    adding to the work's luminosity.

New York City bedecked, ornamented, and flag-bespangled—
    to imagine the sounds ...
        their own ferocious accompaniment to the sight:
        the wind flap of Union Jack, the slap of tricolor,
        stars-and-stripes wind crackle, a snap of the Canadian Red Ensign.
This patriotic panoply of a gorgeous, golden city day.
Does a bugle call to men hardly more than boys?
Wars' harsh realities are not here.
Here, the glory and the grandeur are on Hassam's
    flag-flown Fifth Avenue.

HEAVY METAL

The metallic whine, that's the 4 train,
tasting the track grit as the subway comes.

In the accelerating tin can, I glance around at
the starers—a short, older man, combing a lush beard,

looking as if he's plotting revolution, muttering,
"*Ryby, ryby.** We're all little fishes."

The crackle of newspapers being thumbed open,
the narcotic of tabloids' sex and gore.

Then amid the *Times'* update of wars and economic noir,
news of extrasolar planets orbiting stars in remote constellations,

unimaginable distances far, these exoplanets and their stars;
how tidy the one progression from "Twinkle, Twinkle"

to school's Calder mobile of our revolving eight
with the then-planet Pluto's handball-sized orb.

The widening parameters of a "comfort zone" for life in outer space,
going by the evocative name "Goldilocks zone."

Feeling a Morse code of the subway's dash and stop,
clattering in a subterranean tunnel,

Squashed into by a beefy platinum-blond,
candidate for a heavy-metal band with her face piercings.

---

* Russian for "fish."

Go back to muse on scientists' prodigal advancements;
hare and hounds to find extraterrestrial intelligence.

Next, climb from the subway into November's gusty overcast;
326 exoplanets discovered as of this month.

Extrasolar Gliese 581d they claim as a candidate for having life,
although nothing seems alien upon exiting the 4.

THE BOULEVARDIER'S DAWN / COCKTAIL HOUR

Pilasters held up the roof of night,
an unusual clement evening shortly past
    the equinox;
about were yet sprinkled holiday
    lights.

Otherwise, Manhattan, awash
    in twilight.

Twilight, a fulsome and savvy blue
    as pumped by an accordionist,
sky the shade of a philosophe—
    subtle, contradictory.

When pilasters held up the roof of night,
    an aperitif of blue, twilight that piques
    the senses,
seemed to dissolve the divide to Paris.

From Lexington Avenue to the Left Bank,
le Deuxieme et Duane Street,
Champs-Élysées and Chelsea.

Booksellers along the Seine,
fringing Central Park, browsing the volumes.

Alors, in twilight, Paris a mere moment away—
    a dip in *le pond Atlantique*.

The pilasters held up the roof of night
beyond the slow-divulging skein of infinity;
the eve moonrise (with its quadrant of frost)
    was marked by propinquity.

Twilight: blue amor, as day seduced starlight.

PICTURES AT AN EXHIBITION: NEW YORK CITY

Echoey Eleventh Avenue,
freight lift to the labyrinth of plaster wall,
Chelsea's vogues to monitor.
Pipes of paintings, diamond-like, mine the gallery.
Gouached, encausticed, tempera-ed,
facets of stretched canvas
to browse: color as element and hue and tint
spectrums of the monochrome,
brushwork, nuanced impasto, drip, and spatter.
To engage with one's eyes, dispel the strabismus of the
    work-a-day
compositions, kaleidoscopic—line, form, mutable perspective
in toto the show, not of representation or abstraction but
    tonalities.
An artist's *glissando*,
the Chelsea warehouse as *tempietto* …
    and the works leaving imprint
        and *tempi*.

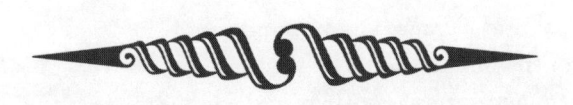

SOME IRREPARABLE LOSS

Shattered cobalt blue upon the kitchen tiles
like gathering shards of a September sky
slivers, chips, the cedilla that was the handle,

having known an expert art historian,
a connoisseur of museum shelves of ancient Greece
gymkhana of black and red figure pottery.

The season when the mechanics of living
seemed all slipped cogs and gears,
a rutted escarpment, the slope of the day

a small storefront window with shapely bowls, vases
that advertised lessons given in the craft,
a whim—or was it an urgency?—for the savor of newness.

The sensation, the language, the techniques
reaching in to *slip*, elation it was to *wedge*,
exhilaration in feeling pliant clay upon the wheel,

a new bond to humankind's mastering civilization,
the genius of achievement in the kiln to bake,
the divine in the impulse to glaze, to decorate.

Revisiting the museum's galleries with another aesthetic,
each krater, each kylix a triumph of mastery,
themes and variations upon paradise's dictum: "to name."

Never beyond an introductory few lessons
but an inordinate pride with my cup's final firing,
an oblation to some power with each morning's coffee.

THE GOTHAMBURG BIBLE

Where the Plesiosaurus in the Natural History is a little tonier,
the Gainsboroughs at the Frick a tad blasé,
a modicum more recondite than the Continental, the cubist at MoMA,
the Metropolitan Museum's Modigliani nude that much more exposé.

Oysters Rockefeller swim in their own element,
the Waldorf Astoria is egged on to poach a Benedict,
and the *ta-mah-toe* and clam marry in Manhattan chowder,
thence the potable and the maraschino bathe in rye and sweet vermouth
    in the town's signature cocktail.

The rain in Spain, foggy London Town, but nowhere else the repute
    to better sell ice to Eskimos
while not the altitudenist, what other skyscraper than
    the Empire State Building legends a lovesick ape?
Then, for the river's span, that swindler's suspension, the veriest
    Brooklyn Bridge.
When the Talk of the Town gets clamorous in a polyglot of tongues—
    the UN—and saris and obis give guide,
the town's only lion's share of Patience and Fortitude at the Public
    Library at Forty-Second and Fifth, and a leonine invite to meet over
    "CATNIP."

Shakespeare stagings to Strawberry Fields / the Boathouse to Bethesda
    Fountain: Olmsted's Central Park for pursuits of man
    and doggy delectation.
Sidewalk's center stage: steel drums, break dancing, rappers, a soulful
    saxophone, a Latin dance band, Peruvian pipes, and a panhandling
    Statue of Liberty mime.
In the *Times*, archaeologists debate which is the most ancient—
    Cleopatra's Needle, the Temple of Dendur, or the joke about the way
    to Carnegie Hall ... *practice, practice.*

To mourn: when sunk to a New Jersey landfill, the Baths of Caracalla,
    the former Penn Station.
Also for the native pedigreed, acoustic and awestruck flatter since
    the old Metropolitan Opera's depart.
The Memorial yet lingers the reflection of the sun upon the silver skin
    of the twin colossi.
That great enlarged Kodachrome that galleried Grand Central Terminal
    before everything became enhanced ... i.e., *hyped.*

Now, magnet to towns, cities, crossroads, villages—domestic
    and across the globe—the glitterway of Broadway
once a Renaissance, to a gilded urban gentrification: the Apollo's talent-
    night contests and Harlem's famed Southern cooking, *going to the grits,*
parade-swept Fifth Avenue and marchers who celebrate rich ethnic
    diversity as they syncopate uptown,
a touch of *la vie boheme*, when Greenwich Village was the haunt of poets
    and artists, and that bongo beat upon the bourgeoisie, the beatnik.

The city's vividness is growing: *Oy!* of the Lower East Side; saints
> and *scungilli* of the *feste* of Little Italy; Chinatown's neon jumble
> of restaurants (or is that a *wonton* number of eateries?).
What's not on the menu at Per Se is saleable on the vendor's cart:
> the salt pretzel, kosher frank, halal kebab.
Behind upper Madison Avenue's sleek facades to the cached boutiques
> of Soho, outfittings on the cutting edge of fashion,
there, she is getting out of a cab: the Russian supermodel of the Slavic
> cheekbones, the African American cover girl with the look
> of a Nubian queen, the Chinese *face*—all severe bangs, kohl-blackened
> eyes, pouted claret lips.
What the boroughs and the tourists voyeur for: celebrities.

Even in 5 a.m.'s filtered dawn in the Wall Street canyons (where heroes are
> feted and those damn Yankees often ride), as a tabloid wind tumbles, its
> day-old headlines yet quip to the bone
in the savvy city, classy habitation: Gothamburg.

CAN YOU HEAR ME, WATSON?

Making a call is the least done on our smartphone.
Betwixt the crank-operated machine and our apps,

there was an interim when, for a time, a slim,
streamlined, push-button device was debuted with

the promotional advert "It's little, it's lovely, it lights."
And, in truth, mirabile dictu, a soft glow was emitted.

This was the Princess phone and, as further inducement,
came in colors to seduce the femme teenager—

a '50s powder-pink, turquoise, or classic virginal-white
New York City's Ma Bell.

Surely, I'm not the only dowager who found for the Princess
another use that, in its way, twins the smartphone of today

and the Kindle or electronic book reader.
At thirteen, I had a lights-out curfew, but books were often

too delicious to put down, and so any number were read by
the glow of the ingenious light in my turquoise little phone.

Possibly, we are in the electronic age—an advanced civilization.
Possibly, too, we didn't know when we had gone just far enough.

THE GYPSY TEAKETTLE

Going-to-seed late-'50s Rialtos, marquees
    spangle Forty-Second Street.
Shorting neon fizzles double features—
    oaters and biblicals.

Already the intermingled rot, theaters
    billboarding triple-X flicks,
schoolgirls in penny loafers dodgy of
    placards with cleavage.

Money clutched for a second-run showing
    of *Battle Cry*,
imaginably to swoon over Tab Hunter
    in marine fatigues.

Stereophonic blood and guts, Technicolor
    (albeit chaste) wartime ardor
only for the virginal, the cinema vérité
    of flickery Hollywood romance.

Movie sated, we exit into the city
    afternoon's warm funkiness,
funds for Schrafft's sandwiches, but
    lured up a second story

to where frowzes of Tintex blonde,
    shellac black, or
a violent henna red will soothsay
    our futures in

the dregs of a gimcrackery china cup of
    tepid tea,

the room's déclassé machine lace and
    leatherette neither Romany nor Delphic.

Still, we're quivery kneed to know the
    auguries of
the sweat-gamy, withered leaf reader
    swirling the lees.

We're in clover—love, money, but for neither
    a future with Tab Hunter.

URBAN LANDSCAPE: THE METROPOLITAN MUSEUM

May Day, when the sun glows energetic upon the tree-shaded paving cobbles,
vendors with an array of prints, artsy postcards, iconic photo reproductions,

a grand uncle from Shaker Heights buys a souvenir watercolor
while on the sidewalk, carts boasting salt pretzels and the Sabrett frank.

About a museum fountain, a nonchalance of private schoolers
are tier-ing up the long flight of shallow marble steps, mesdames, art-goers.

She's a West Sider, tousled brunette with sketch pad, and Lehman Wing bound
cozy of Brits, chatty and vintage Diana.

A trio from Chappaqua doing lunch and Italian portraiture,
they're matched blondes in Fair Isle sweaters, majors in art at Wellesley.

Iranian American of great, almond black eyes here for a talk on Persian painting,
a stunning woman from Dahomey in yellow, green, and white robe and turban.

He's in suit or jeans and backpack
from China's far Canton (Guangzhou) or nearby Connecticut,

and he *must see* the Met's Rembrandts ... van Goghs ...
the medieval armor ... the musical instruments.

A culture-craving mother with stroller-ensconced toddler,
the paired columns of the entryway and beyond—

banners that fly just beneath the pediment advertising exhibits
of ancient Roman glass, Flemish art, Indian miniatures, calligraphy of Japan.

No Daumier of today for the Met's tableaux?
Surely a scene able to be captured (or has been) by a Red Grooms.

The picture outside the picture galleries within.

PHOTOMONTAGE: BLEECKER STREET

Gauzy ceiling of smoke hovering beneath the stamped tin
   —Ballistic missiles in equipoise

Walls glazed ochre by tobacco, and from habitués,
    a gilding of cannabis
   —Cover story in the post-Sputnik era,
   "Why Johnny Can't Read"

Pungent, foamy cappuccino
   —Vice President Richard Milhous Nixon in Moscow
   for the Kitchen Debate with Nikita Khrushchev

Rack of dowels holding *Le Figaro*
   —Generation gyrating to a close with a hula hoop

Discs of Edith Piaf, Jacques Brel, and the Brit
    Petula Clark (in go-go-boot syncopated French)
    casting a trance.

Under the table on the checkerboard tile, a coarse-woven
    Greek bag jingling tokens for the subway ride
    back to the Rockaways—and she's thumbing again
    A Coney Island of the Mind,

Hullabaloo of guitar cases around the sides of the room,

on the cusp of Vietnam, when the war was
the civil rights movement,

glowering wall posters of Jean-Paul Belmondo and Alain Delon,

rebelling against a parental "booboisie,"
and determined to make art, not cereal commercials,

passing on Ginsberg's gospel,

hungering for travel. Meanwhile, this simulacrum
for a Left Bank, and no intimation destiny
might be with an M-16 to the Southeast Asian jungle
or as a fugitive to Canada.

A murmurous cutting of milk teeth on Sartre and Camus
    and, more rumored than read, *Naked Lunch*,
and a plain-wrapped *Tropic of Cancer*
    —the ill-omened, the Pandora's box ...
    advisors sent to the Diem regime.
Counterpoint: a grassy, sweet lull in Greenwich Village.

ELEGY IN A CITY BONEYARD

Suspended in the Caribbean
in a bath of sun-stirred waters,
the infinitesimal deaths of a reef,
coral branch as memento mori.

This urban flux, this tumbrel,
moon-tethered, fluctuating isle,
hurly-burly tropic, intemperately populous
crenellations in a Sargasso sky.

Elegy in a city boneyard,
to what empyrean do these souls fly?
Earthly immortality an optimal quarter hour
or not, then in perpetuity, atoms' effluvia.

Thy sting is unabated.
Lie about the hereafter, Fabricating Man.

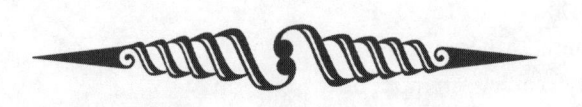

VINCERO

Of rumor: *"Signore, ascolta!"**

On the bill is *Turandot*.
    A necessity of sustaining,
        entr'acte coffee and salmon sandwich
            are taken regimental style—
elbows tucked,
    standing at the Met's
        dress-circle champagne-and-viand
           pedestal tables.
Then a sumptuary pause,
    overheard conversation:
He: "Did you know Callas swallowed
       tapeworms to get thin for Onassis?"
She: "Imagine that love!"
He: "Ruined her voice and beyond,
       arrive Jacqueline."
She: "But for a time ... Callas's incredible
       voice, acting, and beauty."
He: "Onassis wanted for himself a
       goddess the world would worship,
       and that she would die for him!"
She: *[tipping back her flute of champagne]*
       "Vincero."**

---

* *"Signore, ascolta"* is an arching soprano aria from *Turandot*, which Maria Callas made famous and recorded.

** "Vincero"—"I have won"—is, of course, the celebrated bravura tenor aria of *Turandot*, upon morning's coming and the princess not having guessed Calif's name.

THE WORLD'S OLDEST WRITING IN THE TRADE TOWER HOLOCAUST

With the beginning of these tablets, you can say that history begins.
—John Russell, Professor of Art History

When nearly nothing was predictive
   of the horrific attack on the
   World Trade Towers on a
   morning of unsuspect blue,
imaginably, something talismanic
   upon a clay tablet—
quote: *Long after Enlil built the temple
   to Ninlil a great firestorm will come, but
   these words will not perish.*

362 clay tablets and plaques from
   ancient Iraq of 2030 BC
   would survive 9/11.
Sumer, capital of empire.
Looted from South Iraq, the customs service
   received a tip—two boxes of
   "clay objects" out of Syria were
   being smuggled from Dubai
   via Newark.
Sumerians of Mesopotamia.
Customs examined and found the
   artifacts smaller than a
   playing-card deck.
The confiscated treasures went into
   the vault basement of the
   United States Customs House,
   6 World Trade Center.

After the attack on 9/11, it was
    found in the devastation that
    the fragile tablets had been
    water soaked by burst pipes
    and firemen's hoses.
The Tigris, the Euphrates: two
    great rivers of the Fertile Crescent.
The objects returned to the Iraq
    Embassy in Washington, DC, and
    their permission was given for a
    highly delicate restoration.
Eighteen months of conservancy,
    and then Iraq waited until the
    country stabilized before
    repatriating.

Finally, the tablets were at the
    Iraq National Museum in Baghdad.
Some of the cuneiform tablets held
    everyday transactions:
    receipts for goods and services.
Cuneiform: Arrangements of wedge-shaped
    strokes of a stylus on wet clay tablets
    either dried or baked.
Also, deeds, hymns, poetry, literature—
    a diary of what life was like in the
    Sumerian city of Ur in the valley between
    the Tigris and Euphrates Rivers.
But what particularly resonates
    these millennia later is that
    among the cuneiform tablets
    are those with various omens predicting
    the future.
From Sumerians, the *Epic of Gilgamesh*,
    the great flood—and then comes
    the fire next time.

THE ABERRANT STORM

Huddled within a plywood scrim against the
    cresting aberrant storm,

catastrophied houses, tide-swept memories,
    drowned histories, taken lives,
askew—the disordering of existence

like the primal force laid waste,

the scaffold of the submerged world—
    a Luciferian cat's cradle of exploding transformers
pinwheeling, fireballs/gunpowder, black smoke.

Houses burn to skeletal ruin in watery graves,

recalling ... the moon bringer of tides had been at its fullest that night.

Coney Island floats seaward, derelict, macabre Cyclone deaths

For the victims of Sandy
    and the recovery of New York City

recalling ... the moon.

CAROUSEL IN WINTER

A fierce regiment, fiery phalanx,
    the caparisoned charges are close upon
    Central Park West,
dappleds and bays and grays, touched
    with scarlet and royal blues—
fifty-eight ornate, mountable steeds and two
    flamboyant chariots,
horses' arched necks, bits between teeth, stirrups,
    and the merry-go-round's golden poles.

Skeletal overhang of tree branches,
    the winter brown of the lawn,
nimbostratus-dulled sky, and the weather
    report is snowy.
Amusement from the atelier of the Artistic
    Carousel Manufacturing Company,
Williamsburg, Brooklyn, 1908,
    Solomon Stein and
Harry Goldstein's creation—at first
    on Surf Avenue, Coney Island,
fallen into storage until emplaced
    in 1951 as ornaments of Olmsted's design
three-quarter-scale mechanized prancers like a Lilliput
    king's stable.

To ride, to spin, to pump up and down,
    to rejoice in the carousel's music
cymbals and drums, stirring and martial,
    unique to the ear
in the cold air is the merry-go-round's calliope
    clarion.
Even an exotic flourish of wild, striped
    tiger appears
against the day's drabness; this is New York City,
    Technicolor—and the cost: two dollars.

An anecdote in the history of the attraction:
    Jacqueline Kennedy inquired of the
operator if *she* must pay to watch
    Caroline and John ride.

I watch the delight of children
    today attired for the gallop in snowsuits, wool caps,
    and mittens,
the bewitching of a romantic love upon a steadfast
    mount's saddle.
All but the most inclement weather, and the
    merry-go-round
in Central Park, revolves and, revolving,
    resolves some of
the cares of a burdened heart.

TONI

The inaugural sleepaway coincided with that
    epic in Americana, the televised Miss America Pageant,
the ménage à deux or à trois arriving with jammies,
recumbent, ranging the RCA, they readied for the
    avuncular Bert Parks to rhapsodize.

While perhaps a Miss Rheingold was on the
    New York City subways and local beauty queens,
there weren't the rivaling Miss USA,
    Miss Universe, Miss Teen, and the plethora of
    airbrushed supermodels and cotton-tailed
    Playboy centerfolds.
Miss America was beauty *and* baton twirling—
    face, figure, poise, talent.

The tweens rapt, if giggly, picking favorites—
    applauding and booing as the judges
    narrowed the field
absent today's cynicism, advertising for a
    captive female audience.

And nothing went so much with pageant and Parks
    as the Toni home permanent.
By association, with that little kit with its rods and
    chemicals, one would gain not only glossy curls
    but Miss Oklahoma's operatic talent—the "Bell Song"
    from *Lakme*.

The sleepaway has become more raucous.
    Miss America has lost allure ... or is it age?
Things just aren't as Toni anymore.

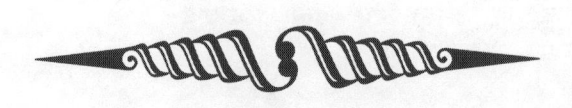

BUSKERS

Jiving the Fifth Avenue corner
        of Bergdorf,
an alto sax is peddling up
    and a blues man
        laying
            down
                a scat line
in the mighty dollary a.m.
                Armani
suit is crossing the pavement
        with Jimmy Choo
and not a dime outta
        Prada
            for "Lover Man,"
so Billy—
        hex their day,
but then Cin-
            cinnati or Seattle
        does a little
finger click,
        gives a listen and a
            fin
        from the tourist,
and man,
        it's sound.

BUBBLE, BUBBLE

Conformist in most regards
yet admittedly wanting *effect*
and open to amicable intervention
otherworldly,

this town's overrun by psychics.
I'll stay aloof from past lives,
leave anticipation to season the future;

however, not gainsaying Shakespeare,
where's the witches?

No confidence in dialing up Wicca,
looking for a consummate conscienceless crone,

there's a shortlist of witchery I'd want,
an enchantment
a mere hex or two.

There are obtainable allurements,
vacancies for reigning princesses—
though time's against me, so somewhere,
keep the caldron lit.

THE FIGURE 5 IN GOLD

Charles Demuth's tribute to William Carlos Williams

integer, integral

5s racing forward in space and receding

versifier, verismo

smell the incandescent clang

the scoping engine eyes

motive, kinetic

splash/gash/splat red

cipher, enciphered

hypnotic, mimetic

fusillade of 5s

pulsate, figurate

glittery, gleaming

power, penta

rays of light infusing

TO JUMBLE

The ATM screen displays characters spelling twenty-five
    different languages
to make a banking-friendly experience of a deposit
    for a Bengali,

just as well a withdrawal transacted in Serbo-Croat.
    Perhaps repressed, I don't attempt

to check my balance or make a transfer to my
    money market in Russian.
For all I know, transliterating, I might be a ruble billionaire.

The parable of the city and its tower is that God's anger
grew at the attempt to build up into the heavens.

God scattered the people of the city upon the earth and
    confused their languages.
Balal in Hebrew is the word for "to jumble."

This gives to English our word *babble*—to talk irrationally,
    crazy talk.
Pieter Bruegel the Elder in 1568 painted his famous
    Tower of Babel, based upon the Colosseum in Rome.

Two hundred years later, the master engraver Gustav Doré gave
another riveting image in *The Confusion of Tongues*.

Go back, perchance, to that far-distant past of 1965,
    a benchmark Boomer year.
Predict that it will be good customer PR at your local
    Chase or Citi.

To have Fukienese to work out your overdrafts,
    babble on

IF, BY CHANCE

The numbers, but within memory,
fantasy, were a shared ticket on the
Irish sweepstakes.

Now billboards blazon a variable
figure in the neighborhood of
a quarter billion dollars.

Not so long past are lottery's beginnings,
and a million-dollar winner
asked if he'd quit his job.

Segue to the commercial, and He is
arguing with She over her
spending winnings on a
pool boy.

The Lotto-carney, an Everyman,
is stopping traffic, silencing
the opera, emptying
the prizefight ring
googly eyed, announcing jackpots.

For tamer types, the scratch-off card
is a matchless experience.

Then, the Mega lotteries, the jaw-dropping,
googol-figured purses with only
half back to Uncle Sam.

'Twas once said no man jumped off a
bridge with a lottery ticket in his
pocket ... presumably, inflation
buoys the survival rate.

DOLCE FAR NIENTE

Oprah raved, and the book is there
    in your lap
as the 20 bus makes its vibrato
    perambulations.

But then with climbers
    aboard,
summer's nonpareil novel
    is put aside.

Ascending the steps,
    into the aisle
a cavalcade of humanity—
    faces to watch.

Long, sweet, dreaming
    to West Fourth Street stop
or at renascent at Tavern on the Green's
    outdoor tables—

or from gallery seating at
    Grand Central's concourse,
a spectacle of passersby: the weaving
    parade

not Veneto surely, or Champs-
    Elysées—not Marrakech
of storytellers and dancing
    snakes.

Suffice this city to hypnotize,
    to lull the axions and dendrites.
Time melts Dali-esque in
    the pursuit of naught.

Naught but the sensation
    of human living
does people watching make
    us humanists.

To Italy's, to France's, to Morocco's
    spellbound—
add that the "city that never
    sleeps" has mesmerized.

THE SAINT'S DAY PARTY

Throughout Bay Ridge, proprietors of jewelry
    and specialty shops look expectant near
    the feast of Saint Rosalie.
Dizzying aromatics perfume from the kitchen
    where *zias* Domenica, Carmela,
    and Annunciata labor.

Pilgrims to the house to pay respects to *nonna*,
    Rosina Felice, on her saint's day,
    expect to be surfeited.
The three zias are pressing sheets of dough
    for manicotti; there will be
    whole roasted lamb and suckling pig.

In an assembly line of Calabrese origin—eons
    older than Henry Ford's—the sisters will fill
    cannolis and cream puffs.
Nonna's two eldest granddaughters, Rose Anne
    and Rose Marie, buff, wax, polish, vacuum
    rooms where a dust mite is as rare as a
    space alien.

Then a hush falls upon preparations
    and a bedroom door cracks open—
    escaping, the sound of
    an Italian radio station.
Nonna makes a slow inspection
    as she heads for her chair;
    and Rose Anne and Rose Marie vie
    to bring her in the living room
    the licorice cup of demitasse.

For an Italian grandmother, *nonna* is tall,
    and she is heavy with many childbirths,
    for a long time sumptuous living,
    and a traitorous body.
Rosina Felice settles into the tapestried wing chair
    and, her leg troubled by diabetes,
    goes upon a leather footstool.

She has light olive skin, small features,
    and she is quite vain—
    including about her wedding dowry
    of a large, square aquamarine ring
    and matching earrings.
Nonna anticipates her afternoon,
    with the footstool; to approach her
    to give the mandatory kiss upon the cheek,
    it is necessary for her visitors to kneel
    upon one leg.
She sips her demitasse.
Mona Lisa's enigmatic smile? Rosina Felice's!
    E bene ... the day of *Santa Rosalia*.

EIGHT O'CLOCK

Was it her Viennese? Like an oiled clockwork,
    she ran upon coffee
mother in a floral robe measuring out
    the Eight O'Clock, the Great Atlantic and
    Pacific Tea Company's ground bean
    in its prideful scarlet sack.
Then I, at age three or four, was first taken—
    chick to her biddy—to those
    disappeared cathedrals of fashion
    Best and Company, Bonwit's, Arnold Constable,
    and B. Altman.
After a morning's try-ons, we'd go
    to Altman's Charleston Garden,
    and she'd order me cocoa or lemonade
    and coffee for herself
but with the injunction to me "Now let's
    sit down like two old ladies over a
    cup of tea."

Unrelenting time, my mother, long since dead,
upon occasion, I go now with a
    lady friend for that most cosseting of
    meals, high tea,
to speak of work and travel, theater seen
    and art galleries visited.

The sandwich of cress or cucumber
is fare more solid than a Communion wafer
    but not by much,
the scrumptious scone with its swirl of
    strawberry jam and topknot of
    clotted cream.
The elixir of Earl Grey, English
    breakfast, or Lapsang souchong
glints its amber stream into the
    eggshell porcelain,
and so near "two old ladies over a
    cup of tea."

THE GRASSHOPPER

A concert pianist and interpreter
of Tchaikovsky, my soigné cousin Christine
was a graduate of Juilliard (*appoggiatura*).

A great favorite of mine, she confided
in me (in every way still a girl)
of her dates, her heartaches, her crushes.

Then she was engaged—
and Jean-Pierre was divine.
The two lovebirds asked me along on an excursion

to New York City at night.
We went to a club to hear
Ahmad Jamal—the great jazz pianist (*glissando*).

I, age ten, went wide-eyed at the sounds of Jamal,
second in influence only to Charlie Parker,
and astonished at the people who came to hear him.

Jean-Pierre ordered, and I was served
in a tulip glass a frothed-topped pale green liquid.

Jamal on the keyboard and the bass
braided their intricate patterns (*fortissimo/pianissimo*).

I lifted the tulip glass and quaffed.
I jammed ... then dipped, and went stuporous,
on my first grasshopper cocktail.

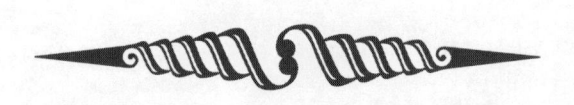

ART IS NOT A BRASSIERE

> *Do not imagine that art is something which is designed to give gentle uplift and self-confidence. Art is not a brassiere. At least, not in the English sense. But do not forget that brassiere is the French for life-jacket.*
> —Julian Barnes, *Flaubert's Parrot*

Narrow brickwork facades trellised
    with fire escapes,
new immigrants seethed with expectancy from
    the shtetl
once, overwhelmed with aspirations
    from Magna Graecia.
Arrive, chic boutiques, cafes that grind-
    to-order beans for a cup of coffee,
apotheoses, storefronts that house fabric
    dealers and zipper wholesalers,
another outpost for the New York City
    art scene. Not the Lower East Side knish;
rather, the LES's nonrepresentation, indebted
    to Kazimir Malevich and Derrida,
paved over the echoes of pushcarts, polyglot din.

In a gallery, a Bulgarian who wasn't an émigré
    until the late Reaganite
is having an opening, and speaks volubly
    about the silences in his paintings.

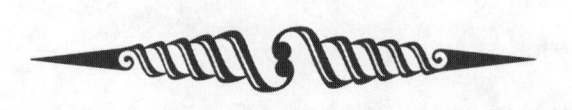

NE PLUS ULTRA

Marking Mimi's launch for Moscow to write a soap opera set in the Crimean War

A femme party this day in the luxe precincts
    of Caviar Russe:
a banquette facing the smoky-azure Russian
    fairy-tale murals,
a flute of a chilled pink champagne to toast
    womanhood,
served two spoons of beluga, shimmery,
    delectable sea pearls.
Savor upon blini, upon toast, upon, yes,
    a sliver of potato,
caviar in a bath of crème fraiche and
    a sprinkle of fresh chives,
explosive in the mouth, and the burst
    is voluptuous.
My, but the ladies in question today are
    sybarites.
Then a portion of smoked salmon melting
    like butter on the tongue,
gourmandizing, splurging feeds more
    than physical hunger.
A maître d' comes to the table to further
    cosset them.
He hovers; they'll have warm, buttery blini
    to enfold salmon morsels,
this "Hermitage of an Eatery," this refuge
    from pedestrian dissonance,
an afternoon like being dropped into a celebration
    by Tolstoy.
The ladies, writers, sally forth to pen
    luxuriant prose.

REVERIE

An upstairs room that serves a high tea
is all chintz and cabbage roses and passementerie.

Cucumber sandwiches with the crusts cut off,
A hurricane shade dims the light soft.

A complex oolong or a flute of champagne?
Deciding on a cherry-stem tisane.

The city's Klaxon is shuttered, halt,
a distant confetti blowing the asphalt.

A truant from matronly vocations
wrinkles potions and taxpayer obligations.

A smidge of strawberry jam for the currant scone,
a morsel of sugar-sweet delectation known—

piquancies beguiling so delicately
falling into a state of quixotry.

In full knightly armor, you materialize,
and I'm castles in Spain in the skies.

Noble sir, you adore me, you my flirtation.
This madness à deux lasts as long as libation.

A worldly waiter conjures the addition,
urban time-card punches inhibition.

Still, Lucullan pleasures stirs the juices,
knowing tasteful titillation's uses.

A semidomesticated male can here be bombastic,
so dining out on make-believe's fantastic.

BARCAROLE

He, born under the sign of Leo, who must be feted
    in the *once upon a time* of Tehran, Iran.
She, born a Libra, a wife's delectation,
    tho' she needs to call upon viziers.
Shah on the Peacock Throne appears dynastic;
    years before overthrown,
a breakfast cart is wheeled to a room in the Hilton
    with a panorama,
sprawled white city, pierced by turquoise domes,
iced confection of cake and chilled champagne
for a birthday revel prefatory to a drive
    to famed archaeology, Persepolis.
O Cyrus, O Darius, we come bearing this news
    after 2,500 years.

A revolution's time lapse to Central Park, New York City,
a deck with aquatic view and two rum Tom Collins,
sultry, late summer at the boathouse, *her reserve*
fare American, prefatory to a placid gondola's ride
    on the lake,
our gondolier passing under a stone bridge,
    the *cantare*'s birthday song—
felice, echo, *compleanno a lei*, echo, *felice, felice*.
O Frederick Law Olmsted, we come celebratory,
    travel sated, but not jaded,
        enjoying his felicitous natal day.

URBAN HOMESTEADING

A jab of chemical,
    the handyman Brassos, the entrance railing

bricks in rusty-red registers,
    punch-holed with reflective window ports,

the polar masquerade of air conditioners
    in flush-set oblongs.

Step down into a checkerboard lobby
    with a dusty savanna of planter ferns

Once, Conestogas drawn by yoked oxen
    cut a pioneering swath of track

across plains—
    the loam so fertile, rich, and depthless.

Now, a prewar Otis (numerously mechanic-ed),
    hoists upward a dozen floors,

urbanite paranoia of locks
    keyed open to the welcoming familiar,

a cubby of an apartment's refuge
    from a native's love-hate relationship

with strumpet-goddess Manhattan,
    her extremes of wealth and want,

her million price-tagged opiates
    against life's capricious transience.

BLIZZARD DAY: NEW YORK

It doesn't fall—it pounds itself
crystalline white wall descended,
the skyscrapers rising up from
the snowbanks like Legos,
momentary luminescence, the crust's crunch.

Sounds of the city in snowfall
muffle or grow tinny thin.
Then comes the grating noise
of the unmucking metropolis,
the Department of Sanitation's
mechanized onslaught.

Finally, it's glazed grime—a floe with
cigarette butts down the gutters.
Once pristine, in pockets around the tree planters,
a dog peed,
numbing puddles at the curbs.

Then it's all memory and
salt bleach on the sidewalks until
the meteorologist's awaited next
gloomsday report (except for
the children, for whom it's been
snow, beautiful snow, sno' school).

THE BIG BANG

Some enactments come with a caveat:
a gun will be fired at this performance,
beware, Lisel shall murder Liselotte;
the stage directions demand conformance;
the plot machine has its devices;
at curtain call, our heroine arises.

Not all life's theater gives warning
a gun will be fired at this performance.
Varied machinations are aborning.
A dramaturge devises a play's adornments.
Let the audience yen surprises.
Death comes in sundry guises.

Existence is but an entr'acte.
A gun will be fired at this performance.
The prime mover merely autodidact,
this mise-en-scène only torments,
plodding minds meaning surmises,
fool's genius absurdity realizes.

OUR TOWN

Cat's paws leaving their imprints
    on the sidewalk,
ladies shod by skyscraper
    engineers

pooling of feet on Forty-Sixth
    off Broadway
when with the abracadabra
    of the Nederlanders,

of Disney, of Jujamcyn,
    of the Shuberts
it is a night of marquees,
    billboards

all to advertise entrée
    into the *the-a-tah*.
Escapist/realist/revivalist/
    cutting edge,

star-studded/ingénue/
    method/Adler coached
Yale tryout/imported
    via Hollywood,

attending, we are descended
    from the ancient Greek chorus
or spoken to, perhaps, through
    the imagined fourth wall.

We may exit wrung out or
    whistling,
provoked or cavorted, bored
    or blaspheming.

Minerva's mural on the ceiling,
    the Broadway production
has the klieg light of all
    Times Square.

THE *BRANDENBURG CONCERTOS:*
SNOWY MANHATTAN

Whirling dance of snow flurries
serpentining the park's drive to Lincoln Center,
on the divide has been left a bicycle.

The bicycle's sheath of ice and icicle
like Jack Frost's ten-speed,
Bach's music soars the mind to a higher place.

Fears of cycles of terror—a young North Korean
    tyrant has killed his uncle and advisor,
a spirited chase: the dramatic arc from first concerto
    to last.
Unpredictably, the world is smaller from an execution
    in far North Korea.

Sole ruler/virtuosic soloists, soullessness/scintillating
    starvation/Johann Sebastian—
one restraint less to launch a missile with a warhead;
    playing with annihilation,
driven frozen pellets into which we exit Alice Tully Hall.

Local broadcast journalism covers Macy's extended hours,
    those of Toys"R"Us
theoretically—SpongeBob SquarePants's tricycle this year's
    must-have.
Security steps in at a festering dispute at Target.

The Bach concertos—supreme examples of Baroque instrumental
    music—were once valued at only a few cents (four groschen)
    each.

Dennis Rodman organizes in the isolationist
    and totalitarian state of North Korea, a
    basketball game for leader Kim Jong-un's birthday.

A total glacier in relations, the US/North Korean diplomatic
    Dennis Keith Rodman, notably, is the single visible link.

The *Brandenburg Concertos* offer a consummate chance for
    interpretation, like great Shakespeare.

TWENTY-FOUR-DOLLAR REAL ESTATE

Sluiced from the plane into the terminal,
    impatient to breathe unpressurized air,

swarm outside for a ride in hobbled traffic,
    Queens bathed in cars' noxiousness and hum.

The vertiginous bridge route over the East River,
    there in the sunlight skyline, Manhattan

scissoring haphazardly into the milky sky,
    glint, thrust, vaunt

colossi footed in bedrock
    (archi)tectonic,

a mirage island of every trade route
    postindustrial caravanserai,

evidencing its acme and polyglot—
    quintessential metropolis.

THE CITY KAROOMS ACROSS MY BEDROOM WALL

In the yellow of stinging bees, rain slickers, and
    black-eyed Suzie's petals,
a taxicab is racing nighttime to a metered destination
    for the right-side
photograph; hindquarters foremost, a monocular-eyed
    hack
is haunting center-ground, a ghostly stalagmite
    skyline,
a rocket-like silhouette tower, within its spheres
    of influence.
Scene left is pinioned by a detective blue squad car,
    red summoning roof lamps
driving away toward the crime and criminals of the
    Brobdingnagian town,
dishing up this camera shot of Manhattan, a dominant
    half-dollar.
Con Ed's manhole cover adds its argent to this tableau
    like a spun disc.
Within the walnut frame and the fat white mat, a half-lyric
    then
"… make it anywhere, New York" pixilates the contours
    of the room.

PORTRAIT

Passegiata, a noontime circuit of my city blocks—
presto, the light changes, and the promenade halts
alongside as the crosstown traffic guns.
A boy with a ferret on his head
I ask: the boy's Bob, and the ferret (with his tiny
    collar and leash) is Jack.
He's a great pet and very smart and, Bob adds,
    likes to be taken for an airing.
The light goes green, and Bob steps off.
I'm suddenly thousands of miles away in Krakow,
    Poland, before
Leonardo da Vinci's *Lady with an Ermine*,
the teenage beauty clasping the golden ermine
    probably Cecilia Gallerani,
the mistress of *il Moro*, Ludovico Sforza, Milan's
    ruler.
The painting, bought in 1800 by Prince Adam Czartoryski
    for the family collection,
has survived, the best of Leonardo's works, after
    five hundred years.
A tootle of car horns brings me back from reverie.
I see that, oblivious to the karooming of cabs'
    and buses' metallic rattle,
Bob walks on amid the lunch-hour pedestrians,
    Jack alert, forward looking on Bob's head
the ferret's tail an undulant S down the boy's
    neck—
boy and ferret, a small urban masterpiece.

VANTAGE

In the cirrus and nimbostratus and the upmost stories
    of the Chrysler Building, Woolworth, World Trade
Manhattanscape is a zebra-ing of architecture and
    roadways alight with talent and traffic signals.
Look-see to the harbor-lands and the flatlands, and the
    outer-lands of Queens,
past Hoboken (oh! surely past), then all of New Jersey,
    westward,
on northward beyond the harp strings of a bridge,
    the geology of palisades, northward ever until
    dissolved from sight, perhaps behind a Catskill
empyrean surfeited with demigods and muses; upon the
    city are such creative urgencies: singularities,
    monumentalities, hybrids of the seven arts.

Stand on this pinnacle vantage—Rockefeller Center,
    Empire State Building—and vaunt, vaunt it.

NIGHTHAWKS (1942)

Edward Hopper

The four are reprised, and unasked, loneliness
diner not much different,
but the snap-brims are only a distant memory,
trademark of the '40s man.
She's unchanged, a redhead in a red dress that shows
    a curve of milky skin.
Then she looks expectant toward the paper-capped
    soda jerk
for a word passed in the emptiness of the blackout
    city.
Who is with her now—who then?
Stranger? Coworker? Friend?
    Lover?
Someone to make the night pass over a cup of coffee.
The solitary male figure hunkered on his diner stool—
lost in thought, observer jealous, or the other guy
    a fool?
To imagine she'll be as approachable come
    work-a-day sunrise,
that counterman who wouldn't trade his job
    in the small hours
when the stories he hears get long, and sometimes
    the tips big for a brew.

The only things holding back the Stygian gloom
are proximity, the four-square diner's architecture, and joe.

FERRIES

We rode the ferry in the clasp of a harvest moon—
the Staten Island ferry—
and it was a dreadnought
passing Liberty Island, a long kiss
I cuddled and yearned.

Those contradictory hours afloat,
churning New York Harbor,
the shortest, endless voyage
between terminal and terminal,
and seeing no terminus, I blurted,
"I feel immortal!"

Don't tempt fate en route to Staten Island.

The First Cause found cause.
College was done, and
boundless time to decide the rest.
Wow! To be at liberty in Manhattan.

And the torch I carried

Surely situated now in middle age,
freighted with regrets
while luckier in later love than deserved,
I do not dread death.
Charon and the Staten Island ferry both charge.

I only need to coin an immortal passage.

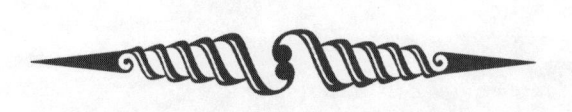

RAIN TATTOO

Hard rain today, so
the jerky stop-start taxis
seem to stipple
the asphalt roadways with chrome yellow.

The street dealers mummify
with plastic sheets all
their faux Vuitton, Rolex, and Armani.

Thén, as it turns to downpour,
in the doorways mushroom
umbrella entrepreneurs
(whether more to be studied by
mycologists,
meteorologists,
or investment bankers).

I, this day, am cozy,
also unsheltered, purposeless
because it was for you.
All the sensations I'd hoard,
remembered hours when,
in New York City,
the skies emptied—
eclipsed by the
emptiness of losing you.

Edwards Brothers Inc.
Ann Arbor MI. USA
November 27, 2017